Storms

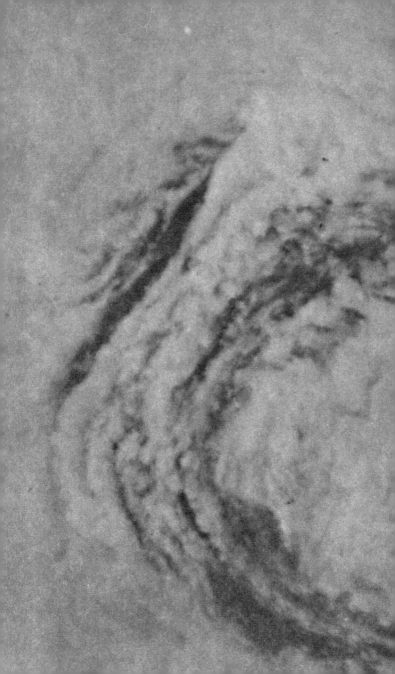

STORMS

Their Origins and Effects

by Paul E. Lehr

illustrated with photographs
and with paintings by
Harry McNaught and Nino Carbe

 GOLDEN PRESS • NEW YORK

EDITORIAL ADVISORS

JOSETTE FRANK, Director for Children's Books,

Child Study Association of America

DR. LELAND B. JACOBS, Professor of Education,

Teachers College, Columbia University

CREDITS

ESSA (Environmental Science Services Administration), 64, 65, 67, 73
Rapho-Guillumette, Christian Cambazard, 74
Independent Protection Co., Inc., Goshen, Indiana, 38
National Aeronautics and Space Administration, 53
New York Daily News, 9, 33
United States Air Force, 3
United States Department of Commerce, Weather Bureau, 6, 8
Wide World Photos, 5, 46
Worcester Telegram-Gazette, 27, 28, 42, 56, 61

TABLE OF CONTENTS

What Is a Storm?

AT every moment of the day and night, many kinds of storms are raging over land and sea. At this very moment 1,800 thunderstorms are spitting lightning, soaking the earth with tons of rain, and flattening crops with hail. Blizzards and other snow storms are whitening parts of the winter hemisphere of the earth. Waterspouts are whirling over the tropical oceans. Somewhere over a lonely ocean current, a hurricane with its awesome winds may be forming. In New York, people may be looking at a cloudless sky, while less than a thousand miles away other people are sheltering themselves from a storm.

A storm is a disturbance of the atmosphere. It is made up of such elements as strong winds, rain, snow or hail. During some storms, winds and flooding cause great damage. During a blizzard, snowdrifts pile up and block roads. Ice storms snap telephone and power lines, and break branches off trees.

A tornado, the most violent of storms, may pass over a town in a few minutes.

Its violent winds can uproot trees, demolish houses and take lives. Tornadoes have torn wool from grazing sheep and plucked feathers from chickens. Once a man was sucked through an open window and left hanging over a branch in a nearby tree. Stalks of wheat have been found driven into trees. A 700-pound refrigerator was found 3 miles from the wrecked house out of which it had been lifted. A small boy awakened to discover that his bed had been whisked out from under him by the wind. A train engine was lifted from its rails and set down on another track headed in the opposite direction.

The wind speeds of a tornado frequently reach 200 miles an hour, and are sometimes as strong as 450 miles an hour. The con-

Houses have been demolished by tornadoes.

Hurricane winds cause enormous waves.

trast between a tornado and a hurricane is great. The hurricane is a massive, slow-moving storm. Often a hurricane stretches 400 miles across—about 2,000 times wider than the average tornado. The large size and slow movement of a hurricane make prediction of its path possible. But the pin-point size and short life of thunderstorms and tornadoes make prediction of their exact location and direction extremely difficult, if not impossible.

Distinctive clouds and precipitation, as well as high winds, are common to storms. Precipitation is the weatherman's name for rain, drizzle, snow, hail, sleet, and other forms of water falling from the sky.

Clouds are the first sign of a coming storm. The clouds of a hurricane, for example, move in stealthily, signaling the approach of the storm. First come the wispy, veil-like cirrus clouds, gradually spreading a haze of ice crystals across the sky high overhead. The wind freshens, and the clouds darken a little. Then, small fluffy cumulus clouds speed across the sky below the high decks of darkening clouds. Rain spatters fitfully, the wind gradually rises, and the clouds thicken. Then with a full-throated roar, the tremendous winds of the hurricane arrive.

What causes wind, precipitation and different kinds of clouds? Getting the facts about the ingredients of weather makes it easier to understand what a storm is and why it behaves as it does.

Winds

WIND is moving air. Air may stand so still that there is a calm, but most of the time it is moving at least a few miles per hour.

Winds are caused by differences in atmospheric pressure. Although we can't feel it, the atmosphere presses down on the earth with an average force of 14.7 pounds on each square inch. At sea level the pressure is greater than in the mountains. Just as water flows downhill, so air flows from areas where the pressure is high to areas where the pressure is low.

Differences in pressure are caused by unequal heating of the earth's surface by the sun. Where the earth is heated strongly, the air above it is warmed and becomes lighter. So the pressure decreases. Where there is no heat from the sun, as happens at night, the air cools and becomes heavier, so the pressure increases.

At the seashore, the sand absorbs heat from the sun, and warms the air above it. The sea, however, reflects most of the sunlight, so the air above the water is warmed only a little or not at all. As the warm,

Valley breezes in daytime, mountain breezes at night.

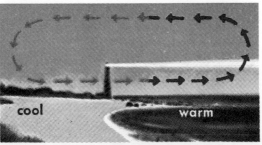

Sea breezes in daytime, land breezes at night.

light air above the sand rises, the cooler, heavier air over the sea flows onshore. This wind is called a sea breeze and shows, on a small scale, the typical flow of air from high pressure (over the sea) to low pressure (over the sand).

The winds over the earth behave much like the sea breeze, blowing from high to low pressures. Regions near the equator receive more heat than the polar regions. So a belt of low pressure forms near the equator and one of higher pressure forms near each of the poles.

Because the earth rotates eastward, winds blowing toward the equator are turned toward the west, while winds blowing toward the poles are turned toward the east. The rotation of the earth also causes the belts of high and low pressure between the equator and the poles.

Most storms are found in low-pressure areas, or "lows." The winds blowing around a low turn counterclockwise in the northern hemisphere, while winds of a high-pressure area (a "high") blow clockwise around it. Since most storms move from west to east,

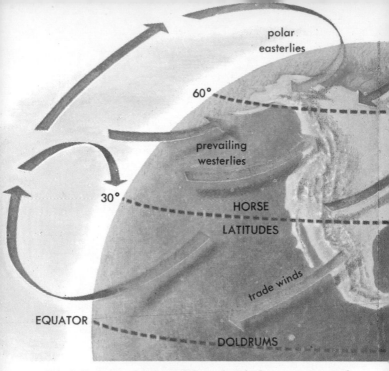

Wind directions in the northern hemisphere are mapped here. Air rises over equatorial region, moves northward, and sinks over polar region. Rotation of earth deflects southward-blowing winds toward west, and northward-blowing winds toward east.

the very first sign of a storm in the northern hemisphere is a south wind. As the low-pressure area with the storm passes over, the wind shifts from south to west to north.

Weather vanes are the oldest weather instruments known. They show wind direction by pointing into the wind. An instrument called the anemometer has been

14

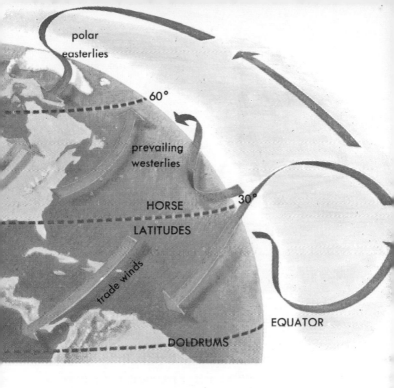

developed to measure the speed of the wind.
At airports and at weather stations you can
see the revolving cups of the anemometer
just below the weather vane. When there
is no wind the cups stand still. When the
wind is strong the cups spin rapidly. The
wind speed is recorded electrically.

In 1805, Admiral Beaufort of the British
Navy invented a system of estimating wind
speeds. This system measured the effect
of wind on the sails of a ship. Beaufort

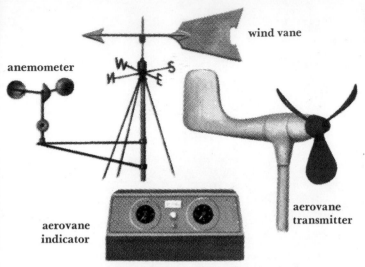

The wind vane indicates wind direction, and the other instruments indicate wind speed.

used numbers from 0 (a calm) to 12 (a wind of hurricane force) to designate wind speeds. This scale has been adopted for use on land also. In the table, Beaufort's number 3 is a gentle breeze (an 8- to 12-mile-an-hour wind) that keeps leaves and twigs in motion. Beaufort's number 9 is a strong gale that breaks tree branches. Wind speeds are given both in miles per hour (mph) and knots, or nautical miles per hour. By international agreement, all wind speeds measured by meteorologists are reported in knots.

ESTIMATING WINDS
ON THE BEAUFORT SCALE

Beaufort number	mph	knots	Description	Observation	Symbols on weather maps
0	0-1	0-1	calm	smoke rises vertically	⊚ calm
1	1-3	1-3	light air	smoke drifts slowly	⊚ calm
2	4-7	4-6	slight breeze	leaves rustle	5 knots
3	8-12	7-10	gentle breeze	leaves and twigs in motion	10 knots
4	13-18	11-16	moderate breeze	small branches move	15 knots
5	19-24	17-21	fresh breeze	small trees sway	20 knots
6	25-31	22-27	strong breeze	large branches sway	25 knots
7	32-38	28-33	moderate gale	whole trees in motion	30 knots
8	39-46	34-40	fresh gale	twigs break off trees	35 knots
9	47-54	41-47	strong gale	branches break	45 knots
10	55-63	48-55	whole gale	trees snap and are blown down	50 knots
11	64-72	56-63	storm	widespread damage	60 knots
12	73-82	64-71	hurricane	extreme damage	70 knots

17

Clouds

CLOUDS are usually the first signs of an approaching storm. Some storms are accompanied by almost every kind of cloud, others have just one kind, and a few have no clouds at all.

Clouds form from moisture in the atmosphere. Even the air of a cloudless sky contains some water in the form of water vapor, a gas. This gas is made up of particles so small that they are invisible. At a given temperature, the air can hold only so much water in this invisible form. If the air is already holding as much as it can, and the temperature goes down, some of the water vapor will condense to form water droplets. Billions of these very small water droplets make a cloud. If the temperature is well below freezing, the clouds may be made of tiny ice particles.

All clouds consist of countless billions of water or ice particles that are carried along by currents of air. What happens to clouds is an important part of the story of storms.

Clouds can be divided into four families. First is the family of high clouds, including

Cirrus

Cirrocumulus

cirrus, cirrocumulus, and cirrostratus. These are clouds made of ice crystals. They are usually found at altitudes of 20,000 feet or higher. Cirrus clouds are wispy and feather-like. Cirrocumulus clouds are thin and patchy and form a "mackerel sky"—so called because the clouds resemble the patterns on a mackerel's back. Cirrostratus clouds form thin sheets or layers. Quite

Altocumulus

Cirrostratus

often a halo is seen around the moon or sun when cirrostratus clouds cover the sky.

The middle cloud family has two members: altocumulus and altostratus. They are seen at heights from 6,500 feet to 20,000 feet. Altocumulus clouds are often seen as rows of whitish or grayish clouds covering much of the sky. Altostratus form a sheet or layer of clouds made of droplets of water.

Altostratus

Stratus

Stratocumulus

Nimbostratus

Cumulus   Cumulonimbus

The low cloud family consists of stratus, stratocumulus, and nimbostratus. Stratus makes a low-lying, sheet-like cloud. Stratocumulus are usually seen as long rolls of clouds covering nearly the whole sky. Nimbostratus are dark, ragged clouds that usually have rain or snow falling from them.

Members of the fourth family are the tall, vertical clouds. These are the cumulus and cumulonimbus. Cumulus are the white, fluffy clouds that you see on a fine day. Where a thunderstorm is brewing you see cumulonimbus clouds. The top of a cumulonimbus will often reach 50,000 to 60,000 feet. It can reach as high as 75,000 feet.

Rain and Snow

THE water droplets or ice crystals which make up all clouds are almost unbelievably tiny and light. The pull of gravity on these tiny droplets is so slight that it would take 16 hours for a cloud droplet to fall half a mile. But even this light pull is balanced by the upward motion of air under most clouds. That is why cloud droplets do not fall.

The average raindrop contains almost a million times as much water as a cloud droplet. This means that a cloud droplet must grow to a million times its original size to become heavy enough to fall as rain. The process by which cloud droplets grow is called "coalescence." This means "growing together into one body." Coalescence may occur in several ways.

The droplets in a cloud are of different sizes so they move at different speeds. When they hit each other, the large drops absorb the small ones, and finally become large enough to fall as rain.

Another type of coalescence occurs when tiny ice crystals and water droplets are present in the same part of a cloud. Some of the water droplets evaporate and become water vapor. The water vapor freezes onto the ice crystals. In this way the ice crystals grow until they are heavy enough to fall as snow or ice pellets. As these fall through the warm air closer to the earth, they melt and become raindrops.

Another cause of coalescence is electricity in clouds. Most clouds have either a positive or a negative charge of electricity. But a thundercloud has positive charges in some parts and negative charges in others. Air currents will sometimes mix these different parts of the cloud so that

Coalescence

cloud droplets with different charges come next to each other. Droplets with a positive charge are attracted by droplets with a negative charge just like two magnets. When the droplets with different charges come together they form a larger drop. These drops eventually grow large enough to fall as rain.

Snowflakes are crystals of ice. All snowflakes are six-sided, but no two are exactly alike. They are formed when water vapor crystallizes on a microscopic bit of airborne soil, rock, or volcanic ash. However, the cloud temperature must generally be between +10°F. and –4°F. before snow will start to form.

Sleet and freezing rain occur when rain, formed in warm air aloft, falls through a cold layer of freezing air. So-called "glaze" forms when very cold rain falls on cold surfaces and freezes instantly. An ice storm can coat the countryside with tons of ice. Trees, telephone poles, and power lines crash to the ground, leaving people without lights, telephones, or heat.

Sleet consists of ice pellets. These are tiny beads of ice, usually not more than an eighth of an inch in diameter. They may be clear, but usually they are cloudy white.

Hail is one of the hazards of a thunder-

No two snowflakes are exactly alike.

storm. Hailstones vary in size from about ¼ inch in diameter to more than five inches. We do not know the exact way in which hail grows to such a tremendous size. But we do know that hail begins to form as frozen raindrops high up where the temperature is well below freezing. More is written in the newspapers about the great damage caused by tornadoes, but hailstorms actually cause more losses, year in and year out. In 1951, the worst hailstorms on record in the United States caused more than $75,000,000 damage to property and crops. The worst hailstorms in the United States occur in the Great Plains.

An ice storm damages power lines and trees.

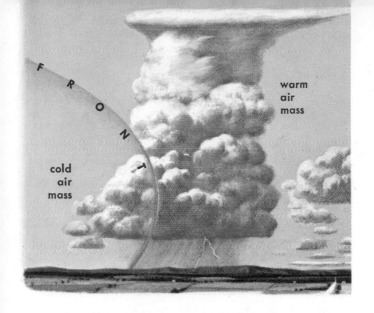

cold air mass

warm air mass

Fronts and Frontal Storms

WEATHER reports mention "highs," "lows," cold fronts, warm fronts, and air masses. A high-pressure area, or "high," is a whirling mass of air which generally moves slowly from west to east. Between the highs are found the low-pressure areas, or "lows," into which the winds blow. In these lows are the unsettled weather and storms.

A *front* is formed when a high-pressure area of cold, heavy air (a cold air mass) overtakes another high containing lighter, warmer air (a warm air mass). These cold and warm air masses do not mix. The colder

29

mass of air pushes under the warmer air and lifts it. Where this happens there is a weather front. As the warmer air is lifted along the cooler front, the moisture in the warmer air condenses. This results in clouds, and often in rain, sleet, hail, or snow. Thus a front brings stormy weather.

As the colder mass of air advances, it forms a cold front. When a typical cold front moves into an area, there is first an increase of winds from the south or southwest. Then altocumulus clouds appear to the west or northwest. The air pressure drops.

As the front draws closer, the clouds lower, and towering cumulonimbus clouds move in overhead. A spattering of rain starts, and becomes heavier as the wind increases and shifts to the west or north. Sometimes there are rain squalls and strong, gusty winds. With the front directly overhead, the barometer shows its lowest pressure. As the front moves away toward the east, the air clears rapidly, the barometer rises, and the temperature drops. Winds become steady from the west or northwest.

A squall line moves in ahead of a cold front.

If a cold front is moving fast, it may be preceded by a squall line. This is a line of black, threatening cumulonimbus clouds with tops rising to heights of 8 to 15 miles. The storms in these clouds may be incredibly violent. All aircraft avoid them if possible. A light plane could be torn to pieces in a squall line. From the ground a squall line looks like an advancing wall of boiling black fog. Rain, whipped about by the wind, pours down in sheets. Flash floods often result, and dry ravines or gullies may become filled with raging torrents.

When a warm mass of air advances, it forms a warm front. Warm fronts move about half as fast as cold fronts. The rainy weather accompanying them usually lasts much longer but is less violent than cold-

31

front weather. Warm fronts announce themselves as much as two days in advance. The first sign is the appearance of cirrus clouds high overhead. As the front approaches, they change to cirrostratus clouds. If cumulonimbus clouds appear, this means that the warm air is unstable. Unstable warm air rises faster than stable warm air, causing spotty rains and thunderstorms well ahead of the front line. If the warm air is stable, steady rain falls from a leaden sky overcast by altostratus and nimbostratus clouds. When the front passes, the rain stops, the sky clears, and the air turns warm. Warm-front weather is not considered stormy weather, unless there are thunderstorms. The steady rain of a warm front is the kind a farmer likes best.

A warm front moves in over a cold air mass, forming a typical series of clouds.

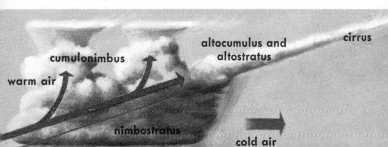

Thunderstorms

A thunderstorm is one of the most awesome sights of nature. Prehistoric man trembled at thunder and lightning. To him the sound and fury of the storm meant his gods were angry. Many primitive people today believe a thunderstorm is supernatural and look to their witch doctors for protection. Even the meteorologist, with all his knowledge of the how and why of a thunderstorm, stands in awe of this tremendous outburst of power in the skies.

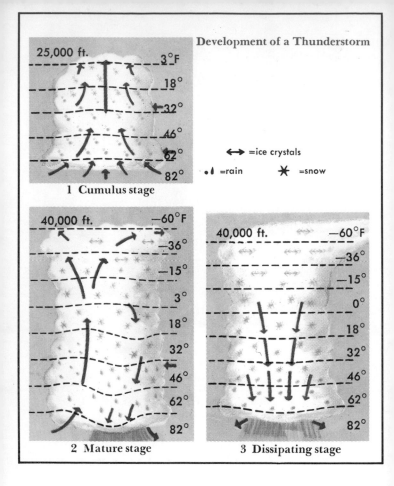

Development of a Thunderstorm

25,000 ft.
3°F
18°
32°
46°
62°
82°

1 Cumulus stage

↔ = ice crystals
• ◖ = rain
✳ = snow

40,000 ft.
−60°F
−36°
−15°
3°
18°
32°
46°
62°
82°

2 Mature stage

40,000 ft.
−60°F
−36°
−15°
0°
18°
32°
46°
62°
82°

3 Dissipating stage

The base of a thunderstorm is usually in the warm, moist air close to the ground, while its top, which can tower as high as 75,000 feet, is up where the temperature is 60 to 70 degrees below zero Fahrenheit. The bottom of the cloud is made of liquid

34

water droplets; the top consists of ice crystals. Within the cloud there are violent updrafts and downdrafts. These columns of rising and falling air can toss an airplane about and even wreck it. Downdrafts reaching the ground spread out to give us the cool, gusty wind that blows just before a thunderstorm arrives.

The thunderstorm itself is made up of several cumulonimbus cells. Each cell is a smaller cloud that becomes a larger cumulonimbus cloud. The development of each cell can be traced through three distinct stages. The *cumulus stage* is first. The diagram shows the rain and snow in this cell, the updrafts, the temperature at top and bottom, and the height—25,000 feet. Next is the *mature stage*. Here there are both updrafts and downdrafts; rain and sometimes hail are falling. The top has reached 40,000 feet and has a temperature of –60° F. Then comes the final or *dissipating stage* of a thunderstorm cell. All air currents are moving downward, the rain has become light or has stopped, and high-level winds blow the ice crystals at the top of the cloud into the typical anvil shape.

Distribution of electrical charges in a thundercloud.

Lightning is caused by the attraction of unlike electrical charges. A thunderstorm cloud has a positive charge near the top and a negative charge near the base. The charge on the ground under a thunderstorm is positive. Since electricity flows from negative (–) to positive (+), a lightning stroke can go from the cloud to the ground or, within the cloud, from the base to the top. Lightning occurs when electrical pressure between parts of the cloud, or between cloud and ground, becomes high enough. Cloud-to-ground lightning starts with a thin "leader" stroke to the ground, followed almost instantly by a heavy return stroke from the ground. What we see as a single lightning flash is actually many back-and-forth flashes from cloud to ground, and ground to cloud, within a small frac-

Lightning is attracted to the highest objects on the ground. For safety, avoid any high objects.

tion of a second. Fortunately, about 65% of all lightning strokes are within the cloud and never reach the ground at all.

The power of a single lightning flash is tremendous. In the average home the available power is about 11,000 watts. A single lightning flash may discharge up to three trillion watts, but this happens in such a short time that there is no way to use this tremendous energy.

Lightning tends to hit the highest object on the ground under the storm. This object can be a church steeple, a house, a television antenna, a tree, or even a man standing in an open field. When a storm is overhead,

Heat from a lightning bolt causes violent
expansion of the air often resulting in destruction.

objects that jut above the ground surface
give off a concentrated stream of positive
charges (point discharge), which attract
the negative charges at the base of a cloud.
The lightning is attracted to the point near-
est to it. Benjamin Franklin studied point
discharge and saw that high rooftops, trees,
and steeples were nearly always the targets
of lightning. So, he reasoned, if he could
"catch" the lightning before it hit the roof
he could lead it to the ground without harm
to the building. He did this by erecting a
pointed rod with its top four or five feet

higher than the roof and its bottom end well grounded in damp earth. The first lightning rod invented by Franklin was installed in Philadelphia in 1753.

Thunder is caused by lightning. A flash of lightning heats the air in its path to about 15,000 degrees Centigrade (27,000°F.) in a millionth of a second or less. This heating causes the air to expand. Expanding air rushing outward in all directions causes the sound we call thunder.

You can estimate your distance from a lightning flash because light and sound travel at different speeds. Light travels 186,000 miles a second, while sound travels only about 1,100 feet a second. Thus, you can see the lightning instantly, but the sound of the

HOW FAR AWAY IS THE LIGHTNING?	
Time, in seconds, between seeing the flash and hearing the thunder	The lightning is actually this many miles away from you
5	1
10	2
15	3
20	4
25	5
30	6

thunder travels toward you at the rate of one mile every 5 seconds. Count the number of seconds between the flash and the sound of thunder. Divide the number of seconds by 5 and you will have the distance in miles between you and the flash. You can estimate seconds by counting slowly.

When you hear thunder, remember the flash of lightning that caused the thunder you just heard cannot harm you. However, it can warn you not to expose yourself needlessly to the next lightning strokes. Following are lists of DOs and DON'Ts for your protection against lightning.

Thunderstorms, despite the hail, lightning, and wind damage they cause, do more good than harm. The principal benefit is the rain they bring. A second benefit that few people realize is that thunderstorms help keep the soil fertile. Millions of tons of nitrous oxide, a good fertilizer, are formed by lightning, which causes nitrogen and oxygen in the air to unite. These nitrous oxides dissolve in the rain and fall to the ground to help enrich the soil.

The total energy of a single thunderstorm

is equivalent to that of hundreds of atomic bombs. The harnessing of this energy is still far in the future.

DOs

Go indoors if possible.
Stay in your car, away from trees.
Get under a cliff or ledge.
Lie flat, if necessary, in an open field or ditch.
Stay out of boats and away from the water.
Ground your television antenna.

DON'Ts

Don't stay out on a high, exposed place.
Don't stand under a lone tree.
Don't stand up or work in an open field.
Don't stay near a wire fence.
Don't go swimming.
Don't repair your TV antenna during a storm.

Tornadoes

A tornado is a thunderstorm gone wild. Sometimes a thunderstorm will develop a small, very intense whirlpool near its center. This whirlpool becomes a twisting, whirling funnel cloud hanging from the bottom of the thunderstorm—a tornado.

The violent thunderstorms in which tornadoes occur are found most often in squall lines that form in the warm air ahead of cold fronts. Tornadoes usually move from southwest to northeast but have been known to skip, make U-turns, or even make a circle. The average forward speed of a tornado is 45 miles an hour. Individual tornadoes, however, can remain stationary for a few minutes. Some drift as slowly as five miles an hour. A few have reached a forward speed of 65 miles an hour.

Tornadoes are the most violent and destructive of all storms. A hurricane may be 2,000 times as large as the average tornado, but it is less than half as violent. Fortunately, tornadoes have a small diameter. Their paths of destruction are usually less than a quarter of a mile wide and average only 10 to 12 miles in length. However, the destruction within the tornado path is almost total.

Extremely low pressure is found in funnel clouds. The pressure of air trapped inside a closed house or barn will cause it to explode outward as the partial vacuum of the funnel passes close by. The winds of a tornado may reach 300 to 400 miles an hour but probably average about 200 miles an hour. Updrafts in tornadoes have been estimated to reach the same speed. These wind speeds cannot be measured, but are estimated from the damage they cause. Buildings are reduced to rubble, large trees are snapped like toothpicks, smaller objects are picked up and smashed or carried for miles.

Thunderclouds form.

A funnel forms as
the tornado develops.

Torrential rains, intense lightning, and often hail go along with the strong winds. The large hailstones of a tornado can cause widespread damage. On June 5, 1917, disk-shaped hailstones 6 to 10 inches in diameter and 2 to 3 inches thick fell near Topeka, Kansas. Hail of this size tears holes in roofs, injures people and destroys crops and livestock. The lightning of a tornado is extremely brilliant, much brighter and bluer than in any other kind of storm. At night, or when the bottom of the thundercloud is hidden from sight, these intense flashes can serve as a warning of an impending tornado.

Tornadoes also occur over water, where

they produce waterspouts. They have very much the same appearance as land tornadoes except for the whirling spray of water seen where the funnel touches the ocean. Waterspouts are quite numerous over the tropical oceans when cloud conditions are favorable. People in airplanes flying over tropical waters have seen as many as ten at a time. While tornadoes are always accompanied by thunderstorms, waterspouts are seen most often with well-developed cumulus clouds that have not yet become thunderstorms. Only once in a very great while does a waterspout move in over land. One did move onshore in the Bahama Islands in 1959. It did quite a bit of damage to boats, docks, and beach houses before it moved inland and died out.

The funnel starts
its destructive course.

The funnel sucks up
dust and debris.

A waterspout appears offshore at Solana Beach, California.

Tornadoes occur in many countries of the world, but the United States has a greater number than the rest put together. In the United States, the Central Plains are struck most often.

In the United States, tornadoes and violent thunderstorms are most frequent during May and June. Conditions then are just right over "Tornado Alley," a wide belt through the middle of the continent from the Gulf of Mexico to Minnesota and Wisconsin. Warm, moist air moves northward from the Gulf of Mexico over the broad Mississippi River valley and clashes with cold air coming from the northwest. The unstable warm air is lifted violently, and heavy thunderstorms are formed. If the warm air is unusually unstable and the cold air gives it enough of a lift, the thunderstorms formed develop tornado funnels. Four or five o'clock in the afternoon, the warmest part of the day, is a favored time for tornadoes.

At the start of the tornado season in March, northern Mississippi is hardest hit. In April the area of maximum tornadoes spreads to Missouri, Texas, Oklahoma, and Kansas. During May and June, "Tornado Alley" extends in a broad belt from Oklahoma to southern Minnesota and Wisconsin. July, August, and September are months of less activity over the same area. Sixty-eight per cent of all tornadoes occur during April, May, and June; 21 per cent occur from July through October; and only 11 per cent the rest of the year.

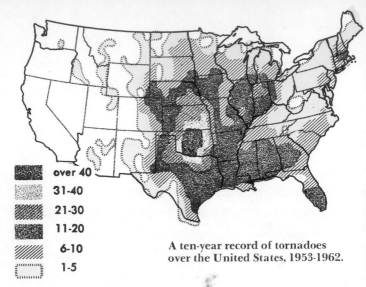

over 40
31-40
21-30
11-20
6-10
1-5

A ten-year record of tornadoes
over the United States, 1953-1962.

If you live anywhere east of the Rock-
ies you stand some chance of seeing a tornado but not much chance of being hurt
by one. In an average year, about 35,000
people in the United States are killed in
traffic accidents. This is over twice as many
as the total killed by tornadoes in the past
50 years.

Tornadoes have been reported every hour
of the day and night every month of the
year. Because of this constant possibility,
the United States Weather Bureau and other
weather services keep a year-round watch
to forecast and warn people of tornado
danger.

48

Tornado forecasting is one of the most difficult tasks for the weather scientist. Today, a great network of surface and upper-air observation stations has made it possible to tell which areas tornadoes are most likely to strike. But it is still impossible to pinpoint just when and where.

A continuous tornado watch is kept at the National Severe Storms Laboratory in Norman, Oklahoma. This center devotes all its efforts toward detecting and forecasting weather likely to produce tornadoes and severe thunderstorms. When such a situation develops, a warning is issued. Radio and television stations alert local residents.

People who live in areas where tornadoes strike should know how to protect themselves. The "cyclone cellar" is one of the safest places to be during a tornado. Many farms in the Middle West states have them. The Red Cross recommends concrete shelters 6 feet wide, 8 feet long, and 7 feet deep. A shelter of this size can hold at least eight people. The door should face northeast, since most tornadoes travel from the southwest. The door must be made of

Cyclone cellar

heavy timber and have a strong bar inside
to keep it from flying open when the tornado passes overhead. A storm shelter is
good insurance. No one has ever been killed
in one.

If there is no storm shelter, the southwest corner of the basement of a frame
house is the safest place. In a house with
no basement, you should go to the southwest corner of the ground floor, away from
windows, and get under a mattress or bed.
Do not remain standing, especially near a
window. Even small objects blown by a
200-mile-an-hour wind can kill.

In the business district of a city, a concrete building with a steel frame is the safest place to be. Flatten yourself against an inside wall on the ground floor. Stay away from the windows. Out of doors, if a tornado is close and coming in your direction, lie down in any depression in the ground. Do not remain standing—even a gutter or curbing can offer some protection.

Hurricanes

"HURRICANE" is the West Indian name for the great tropical cyclones which occur in the Caribbean. They are circular storms averaging 400 miles across. The winds of a hurricane blow at least 75 miles an hour, and often reach 125 miles an hour. The highest wind speed ever recorded for a hurricane was 186 miles an hour (at higher speed the wind gauges blew away). Speeds of over 200 miles per hour have been estimated.

Like all cyclones, tropical cyclones are low-pressure areas. In temperate regions north and south of the tropics, low-pressure areas have both cold and warm air within them. But the tropical cyclone (usually over the ocean) contains only warm, moist air. While a low-pressure area in temperate zones can sometimes be followed right around the world as it moves, the tropical cyclone, or hurricane, usually breaks up as soon as it moves inland.

In this book all tropical cyclones will be called hurricanes. However, these storms are known by many names in various parts of the world. In the western Pacific they are called "typhoons"; in Australia, "willy-willies"; in the Philippines, "baguios"; and in the Indian Ocean, "cyclones." The South Atlantic is the only ocean where hurricanes do not occur.

A hurricane is a giant "doughnut" of clouds, fearsome winds, and heavy rain, with occasional tornadoes thrown in for good measure. It has a center called an "eye." The eye is a clear or lightly clouded circular area that is nearly windless. It is usually about 15 miles in diameter and is surrounded by a wall of clouds which marks the band of the strongest winds of the hur-

In 1958, a U.S. Navy Hurricane Reconnaissance aircraft studied Hurricane Daisy by radar. The airplane was at the bright spot in the center of the photograph.

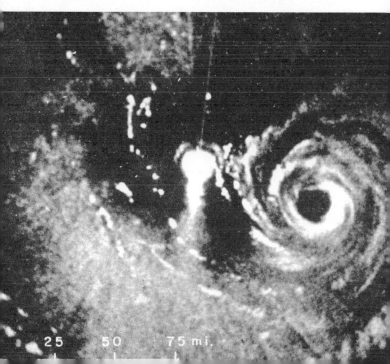

25   50   75 mi.

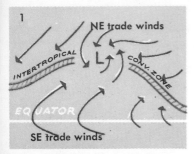

1

NE trade winds

INTERTROPICAL

L

CONV. ZONE

EQUATOR

SE trade winds

Opposing winds in tropical zone
start moist air whirling.

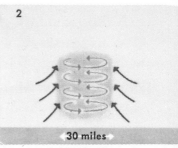

2

←30 miles→

Moisture in rising air condenses,
releasing much heat.

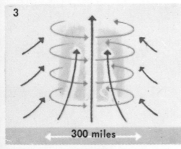

3

←300 miles→

Heat causes whirling air
to rise faster and faster.

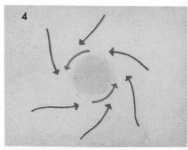

4

Air rushes in violently
at bottom to replace rising air.

ricane. The sudden drop in wind and the
appearance of a sunny sky as the eye passes
often fool people into thinking the storm
is over. Then, as the other side of the hurricane moves in, the storm returns in its
full fury. Weather maps, photographs, radar
images, and flights into hurricanes have all
confirmed this formation. A photograph of
the storm as it appears on a radarscope

shows that it has an "eye" surrounded by spiral bands of rain. A picture taken from an airplane flown high over a hurricane shows an almost perfect circular "eye." The eye is sometimes oval or not completely surrounded by clouds. Some hurricanes have two eyes.

A diagram of a hurricane as seen from above divides it into quarters. The front half and the north side of a hurricane usually have the strongest winds. Thus, in a hurricane moving east to west, the right

Hurricane wind diagram

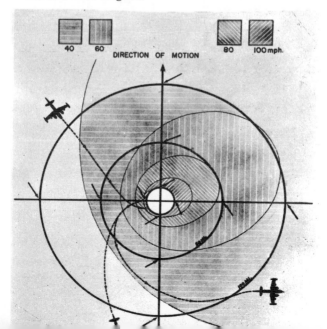

40   60   DIRECTION OF MOTION   80   100 mph.

During a hurricane, ocean waters may sweep miles inland.

front quarter will have the strongest winds. Obviously it's better to have a hurricane pass north of you than south of you. Trace the diagram on transparent paper and move it over a coastal town on a map. Notice how wind speeds and directions change as the hurricane passes over.

Strong winds and storm tides over three times normal height are the destructive forces of a hurricane. The 75- to 100-mile-an-hour winds extend outward from the wall of the eye, cutting a swath of destruction 25 to 500 miles wide. Trees are uprooted, and buildings leveled. The rain seems to blow horizontally, large pieces of debris are carried along, and the unearthly howl of the wind seems to fill the air.

The storm tides and waves of a hurricane cause floods. The storm waves are like very high tides, 10 to 15 feet higher than normal. Sometimes a storm wave arrives suddenly, flooding the coast without warning. Such a wave hit Cuba at Santa Cruz del Sur on November 9, 1932. Twenty-five hundred people lost their lives as the storm wave carried the village away. Winds in this storm were estimated at 210 miles an hour but the storm wave was the main cause of the destruction. Similar waves have been reported wherever hurricanes hit. At the mouth of the Hooghly River, on the Bay of Bengal, 300,000 people were swept away by a storm tide in 1737. In 1864, a storm tide at the same place took another 50,000 lives.

Tremendous amounts of rain fall as a hurricane passes: in 1921, 23 inches of rain fell in 24 hours at Taylor, Texas. At Baguio in the Philippines, a world record rainfall was measured in July 1911. Forty-six inches of rain fell in 24 hours. The total four-day rain for this storm was 88 inches. If this rain had accumulated, the whole town would have been in water 7 feet 4 inches deep. (One inch of rain over one square mile amounts to 17.4 million gallons of water.)

In 1955, a hurricane crossed the North Carolina coast and curved across the Middle Atlantic states, dropping heavy rain over a large area. Close on the heels of the first hurricane, a second moved in, loosing torrential rains over the same area. The disastrous floods that followed took 179 lives and destroyed a billion dollars in property.

Hurricanes are given names for identification. Each year an alphabetical listing is assigned. The first might be "Alice," the second "Betsy," the third "Carol," and so on. The map (on page 59) traces the development of a typical hurricane, which we shall call "Carol". The storm begins west of the Cape Verde Islands. At this stage, the winds are less than 32 miles an hour, so the future hurricane is classified as just a tropical low (L).

As it moves west, the low becomes a tropical storm 6 with wind speeds between 32 and 73 miles an hour. The storm continues to move westward at 10 to 12 miles an hour and the winds increase to hurricane force—over 74 miles an hour. Carol, now mature, crashes into Guadeloupe. Still moving westward at 10 to 12 miles an hour, Carol passes south of Puerto Rico and Haiti, with winds slowly increasing. Then Carol curves north and passes over Cuba and the Bahamas, bludgeoning them

Path of a typical hurricane.

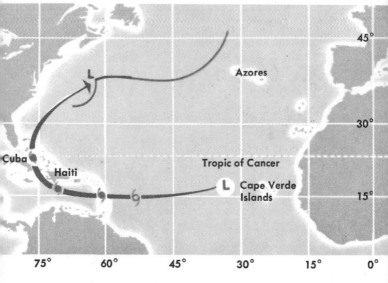

with 125-mile-an-hour winds. The hurricane finally turns, or recurves, to the northeast, speeding up to 30 miles an hour as the wind speed drops rapidly to less than 75 miles an hour. Somewhere north of Bermuda, Carol hits a cold front and eventually ends up as a storm in the North Sea. The path taken by Hurricane Carol is typical of hurricane paths. But hurricanes are unpredictable, and many have taken unexpected courses.

The hurricane season of the Atlantic reaches maximum intensity during August, September, and October. Over 84% of all hurricanes occur in these summer and early fall months. June, July, and November account for 14%, and less than 2% occur during the remaining six months of the year.

For the past 30 years there has been an average of five hurricanes per year in the Caribbean. The greatest number in any one year was eleven in 1950.

In the western North Pacific the active typhoon season lasts from July through November. The Pacific usually has more than 20 typhoons every year.

Signs of the Hurricane

ONE of the first signs of an approaching
hurricane is the storm swell on the ocean.
Waves blown up by the hurricane travel

61

for hundreds of miles, to break heavily upon a distant shore. As the hurricane, still far out at sea, approaches, the tides start to rise. A banded veil of cirrus clouds gradually advances to cover the sky. Finally, an arc of dense clouds appears on the horizon. This is the hurricane itself.

As the storm moves in from the sea, low, ragged clouds moved quickly by the wind—"scud clouds"—appear. An observer on the shore facing the storm sees these clouds move with the wind from his left to his right. The winds are light at first, then gradually increase in strength. The barometer starts to fall, rain blown by gusty winds spatters briefly, then the storm begins. Squalls lashed by violent winds follow each other in rapid succession. The rain comes in sheets, and over all is the deep-throated roar of the hurricane.

A hurricane warning system was established in 1938 by the United States Weather Bureau. Before this warning system was established, 161 lives were lost for every 10 million dollars' worth of property destroyed. In the period 1941–1945, this ratio was reduced to 4 lives lost for each 10 million dollars' worth of property damage. During the August 1949 hurricane in Florida, only 2 lives were lost, while $52,000,000 damage was estimated.

In 1957 Hurricane Audrey hit the Louisiana coast. Despite a warning 48 hours in advance and urgent warnings repeated during the last 14 hours, people at Cameron, Louisiana, refused to leave their homes. More than 500 people lost their lives when Audrey brought in a storm tide of over 10 feet and winds estimated at 150 miles per hour.

Before 1966, when weather satellites began to watch the tropics every day, reconnaissance aircraft constantly searched the breeding grounds of tropical storms. They would spot the storm days before it came near land, and follow its movement continuously. Now the weather satellites send their pictures to the ground by television every two hours. When a tropical storm shows up, a satellite tracks it until it is within range of the reconnaissance aircraft.

This photograph of Hurricane Beulah was taken in 1967 by the ESSA 3 satellite from an altitude of 850 statute miles.

These aircraft, equipped with radarscopes and weather equipment, fly into the storm once every six hours. Reports sent back by the planes tell the exact location of the storm center, the size of the eye, the speed of the winds, and the direction of the storm's movement.

The idea of sending airplanes out to track hurricanes was first discussed seriously in 1937, but was discarded as too dangerous.

Then, in 1943, Colonel Joseph B. Duckworth, an instructor at the instrument flying school at Bryan, Texas, became the first man to make an observation flight into a hurricane. On July 27, a hurricane was approaching his home city of Galveston, Texas, and Colonel Duckworth decided to take a look at the storm. With his navigator, Lt. Ralph O'Hair, he took off in a single-engine two-seater airplane, flew into the eye of the

An ESSA weather reconnaissance aircraft flies over the eye of a hurricane.

storm, and returned to the airbase. In the meantime, a weather officer at the base heard of the flight. When the plane landed, he begged the pilot to take him up for a look. So the first flight into the eye of a hurricane was followed almost immediately by a second flight. At 5:43 p.m. they flew into the eye, and by seven o'clock were back on the ground with the first meteorological account of a deliberate flight into a hurricane.

This eyewitness account proved that most of the dangers of flights into hurricanes were overrated. Before the flight was made, people had thought that the turbulent winds in a hurricane would tear the wings off any airplane unlucky enough to wander into the storm. They also thought that should a plane be lucky enough to reach the center of the storm undamaged, the downdrafts in the eye would surely force it down to the ocean, where escape from the boiling seas would be impossible. On Colonel Duckworth's flight, the turbulence at the level of flight through the storm was no worse than that met outside hurricanes. In fact,

66

Cockpit of reconnaissance aircraft.

it was seldom as heavy. The downdraft in the eye, furthermore, was not strong enough to affect the flight.

In spite of the ease with which Duckworth penetrated the Galveston hurricane, a flight into a hurricane always involves some risk. But after the first flights, more airplanes were sent into the big storms to observe. Penetrations were tried at high levels and low levels, and much was discovered about the kinds of weather to be expected in various parts of the storm.

Low-level flights are made at 300 to 700 feet above the sea. Flying at this low level is very tricky; below 300 feet turbulence is heavy to violent; above 700 feet there will

67

usually be clouds, which interfere with observations. The pilot, therefore, has to fly at a closely calculated height.

As the flight proceeds from the edge of the storm, the pilot flies with the wind. The pressure begins to drop, the winds increase, the sea begins to look rougher and rougher. First a spiral arm is penetrated and there is a heavy downpour of rain for a few minutes. An almost clear area comes next—just before the main edge of the storm appears as a solid black wall. From the wall to the edge of the eye, a distance sometimes as much as 200 miles, the clouds are solid overhead, a driving rain penetrates every chink and crevice, and the sea is a froth of wind-whipped waves.

When the wind hits 60 miles an hour, the pilot heads for the center with the wind on his left rear quadrant. Turbulence has been light but now gets heavier and heavier, until suddenly the plane breaks out into the eye of the storm. In the eye the wind is only a breeze and the sun is shining. But the ocean below seems to boil. Layers of clouds form a high circular wall from the ocean to as high as the eye can see.

The meteorologist reads his instruments and codes his observations while the navigator checks position. Then the radio man sends back the weather information, with the position and speed of the storm. Finally the return trip begins. Seat belts are buckled, everything is fastened down, and the pilot heads for the wall of the eye.

After a brief encounter with heavy turbulence, the flight proceeds out from the storm center. Turbulence decreases steadily, the driving rain gradually falls off, the winds decrease, and the pilot sets his course for the airfield. Throughout the flight a steady stream of weather information has been radioed back to the forecasters. When the weather plane lands, the flight meteorologist and the crew brief the airfield weather staff on the whole flight.

High-level penetrations, made near either 18,500 or 9,800 feet, are quite different. At 18,500 feet turbulence is much lighter than at any other level, but icing can become a great hazard, forcing the plane to seek lower levels. At 9,800 feet the plane flies in clouds much of the time, and encounters more steady turbulence, with occasional unexpected spots of heavy turbulence. At the high levels, the crew uses radar to "see" the storm, and as the plane flies toward the storm center, dropsondes (special measuring instruments) are thrown out of chutes to measure the temperature, pressure, and humidity in the storm. As the dropsonde drifts down on its parachute, it radios information back to the airplane.

By 1945, the military services had trained pilots to conduct regular reconnaissance

The radar antenna sends out signals which are reflected by the hurricane, received by the antenna, and shown as a pattern on the radar screen.

flights to probe hurricanes. The Air Force and Navy have divided the Atlantic into "areas of responsibility" where each keeps constant watch to discover and track tropical storms. In the Pacific the Air Force does this job alone. Despite the rough flying in the hurricane and the thousands of flights made, only three aircraft have been lost since the flight program was started in 1943.

Every possible type of equipment is used to detect and watch hurricanes. Weather satellite pictures are examined closely to determine the presence of a storm. Airborne and land-based radar show the storm at close range. Automatic weather stations on uninhabited islands send back wind and pressure reports. Upper-air sounding reports tell the forecaster what is going on in the high atmosphere ahead of the hurricane.

Even earthquake experts are on the lookout for hurricanes. Their seismographs, or "earthquake detectors," record shock waves traveling through the earth. They can also record microseisms, or very light shock waves, from ocean areas where there are hurricanes.

The age-old cry "Why don't we do something about it?" is raised whenever a hurricane strikes. Something has been done. The hurricane warning system has certainly reduced loss of life. People have suggested that something be done to break up a hurricane before it can do any damage. Perhaps this will be possible 50 or 100 years from now, but our present knowledge shows us no way to "kill" or "steer" a hurricane away from land.

Dr. Irving Langmuir and Dr. Bernard Vonnegut, two scientists who worked for General Electric Corporation, experimented with cloud seeding after World War II. With another GE scientist, Dr. Vincent Schaefer, they found that they could "seed" clouds with dry ice to induce rain to fall, or, using a different seeding technique, cause clouds to break up. This brought the suggestion that a hurricane could be broken up by seeding it with dry ice. Experiments are being planned to find out whether seeding a hurricane will break it up, or at least decrease its intensity.

Others suggested blowing the storm apart

The A-26 Intruder is used in Project Stormfury
to seed hurricanes.

with atomic or hydrogen bombs. But the
energy needed to "run" a hurricane for
one minute is equal to the energy of 1,000
atom bombs, so it would be impossible to
A-bomb a hurricane into oblivion. Also,
atom-bombing a hurricane would make it
radioactive. This would create a great hazard
if the storm moved inland over populated
areas.

The United States Weather Bureau is
carrying on research which may someday
help us fully understand and, perhaps, con-
trol hurricanes. This research is being done
at the National Hurricane Research Laboratory in Florida and at various universities.

Strong winds often accompany snowstorms.

Strong Winds and Bad Weather

OTHER THAN thunderstorms, tornadoes, and hurricanes, there are many kinds of storms and bad weather in different parts of the world. Some of these are so interesting that they are famous everywhere.

One of these is the *foehn* wind, a hot,

dry wind that flows down mountain slopes in many different parts of the world. As the foehn wind blows down a mountainside, it warms 5½°F. for every thousands feet of descent. In North America, the foehn is called a *chinook*. This wind is forced down the eastern slopes of the Rocky Mountains by strong winds aloft. A foehn wind, be it in Austria, Switzerland, or North America, often causes temperatures to rise as much as 30°F. in 15 to 20 minutes. Snow and ice literally disappear in a few hours, either melting or evaporating directly into the dry, hot air. Because of this the foehn is sometimes called the "snow eater."

The foehn is so very dry that it makes the wooden walls and floors of houses dry and split. Furniture comes unglued and everything is brittle with dryness. In the Alpine villages of Switzerland, where most houses are constructed of wood, this dryness becomes a fire hazard. Foehn watchers, or fire watchers, go from house to house to see that all fires are put out and no one smokes. In the Rocky Mountain states, the chinook creates similar hazards but since the wind does not last so long, the fire watch is not so necessary.

Another type of mountain wind that occurs all over the world is the *fall wind.* All fall winds have the same general cause. Surface air cooled by contact with snow or with the cold ground flows downhill from plateaus or mountains into warmer valleys below. Fall winds are so cold that compression does not warm them sufficiently to bring temperatures up to normal by the time the winds reach level land or the sea. The fall winds of Italy and France are the *bora* and *mistral.*

A whole group of cold winds, which have various meteorological causes, are classified as *northers.* The norther of Texas and Oklahoma is a fast-moving mass of cold air that follows a cold front moving southward along the eastern side of the Rocky Mountains. A norther in Texas brings strong north winds, and sudden drops in temperature of 20 to 35 degrees Fahrenheit in as little as two hours.

Many winds carry sand, dust, gravel, or snow. The snow-carrying winds are the *blizzards*. A true blizzard is marked by intense cold, strong winds, and powdery dry snow that is piled by the wind into drifts. Blizzards occur in the interior of continents over such areas as the northern plains of the United States, the central provinces of Canada, and the steppes of Russia.

Blizzards in North America sometimes

A dust storm near Springfield, Colorado, one of the many that swept across the plains of the West and Midwest during the drought years of the 1930's.

have isolated large areas. The great blizzards of November 1958 in the northwest plains states took 34 lives. Food and fodder were airlifted to the thousands of people and cattle that were marooned by huge snowdrifts and the biting cold.

Dust and sand storms are caused by strong steady winds blowing over loose, dusty, or sandy soil. The sirocco, a foehn wind on the north coast of Africa and Sicily, is the dust and sandstorm wind of the Sahara. The *haboob* of the Egyptian Sudan is a dust or sand storm which takes its name from the Arabic word *habb,* which means "wind." This storm, like a wall of sand or dust, often 3,000 feet high, moves across the desert at speeds of 30 to 60 miles an hour. Haboobs can deposit enormous quantities of sand, often burying small villages and caravans trapped out in the desert.

Squalls, too, are found all around the world. A *squall* is a sudden sharp wind, usually accompanied by thunderstorm activity. *Squall lines,* with gusty winds and heavy showers, may extend over hundreds of miles. These lines often form and move across country, well ahead of slowly moving cold fronts, bringing strong winds and drenching rain showers. The gusty strong winds of line squalls and thunder squalls usually blow steadily in one direction. Squalls whose winds have a rotary motion include *typhoon squalls,* a form of waterspout, which gives first notice of its existence by blowing the sea surface into a froth.

The map on this page shows winds and windstorms around the world. There are many small areas that also have special winds, but they are not shown on this map.

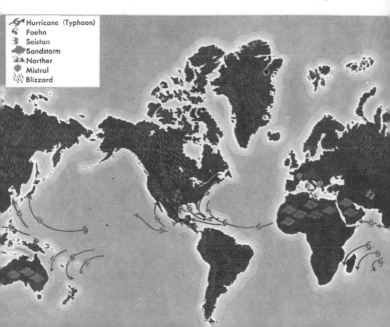

Hurricane (Typhoon)
Foehn
Seistan
Sandstorm
Norther
Mistral
Blizzard

INDEX